Dorset Villages
a guide

by Robert Hesketh

Inspiring Places Publishing
2 Down Lodge Close
Alderholt
Fordingbridge
SP6 3JA
©Robert Hesketh 2022
www.roberthesketh.co.uk

ISBN 978-1-8384668-3-1
www.inspiringplaces.co.uk

Photographs by the author except p.7 left, p.12 bottom, p.17 bottom left, p.20 bottom right, p.21 left, p.24 left, p.33 top, p.39, p.43 top right by Robert Westwood.
Front cover: Top left: Tarrant Gunville, right: Moreton, bottom: Milton Abbas.
Back cover: From top: Symondsbury, Tarrant Monkton, Bere Regis.

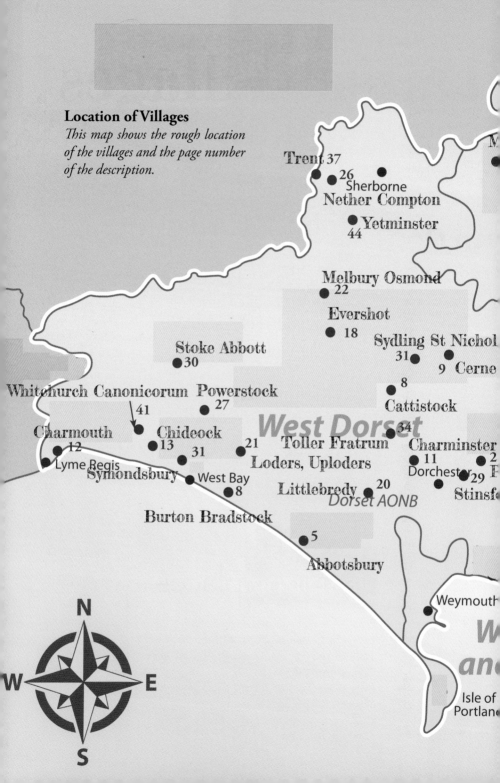

Location of Villages

This map shows the rough location of the villages and the page number of the description.

Trent 37

Sherborne 26

Nether Compton

Yetminster 44

Melbury Osmond 22

Evershot 18

Stoke Abbott 30

Sydling St Nichol 31

9 Cerne

Whitchurch Canonicorum 41

Powerstock 27

8

Cattistock

34

Charmouth 12

Chideock 13 31

21

Toller Fratrum

Charminster 11

Dorchester 2

29

Lyme Regis

Symondsbury

West Bay

Loders, Uploders

Stinsf

West Dorset

Littlebredy 20

8

Burton Bradstock

Dorset AONB

5

Abbotsbury

Weymouth

N
W   E
S

Isle of Portlan

ford
Ashmore
● 6

North Dorset

Cranborne
● 17

set

26 ● Okeford Fitzpaine

The Tarrants
● 34 East Dorset

Milton Abbas
● 23

Wimborne
Minster
30 ● ● 27

Sturminster Marshall
Pamphill

7 ● 42 ● Winterborne Tomson
Bere Regis

Poole

Moreton
● 25

Christchurch
Bournemouth
Poole

Bournemouth

Purbeck

Corfe Castle
● 14

worth
40 ● Tyneham
● 38

19
●
● 42 Langton Matravers

uth
tland

Worth Matravers

English Channel

Introduction

Dorset has many beautiful villages rich in history and a wonderful heritage of vernacular building in a wide variety of locally sourced materials, including stone, cob, brick and thatch. In whittling my original (very long) list of villages down to a manageable 40, I have focussed on those which combine aesthetic appeal with historic buildings, particularly those open to the public, and an interesting story or historical connection.

Some villages, including Abbotsbury, Cerne Abbas, West Lulworth, Tolpuddle, Tyneham and Corfe Castle warrant an extended visit and draw many visitors. Others, such as Toller Fratrum, Whitchurch Canonicorum, Stinsford and Okeford Fitzpaine are little known gems set deep in the Dorset countryside. You may well find yourself the only visitor and share my sense of discovery on finding what they have to offer.

Corfe Castle.

Abbotsbury

Abbotsbury is a large, exceptionally attractive stone built village with a long history and several points of interest. Recorded as Abbedesburie in 946, its name signifies "fortified manor belonging to the abbot". The abbot in question was the abbot of Glastonbury, who long held lands here before the abbey was founded in 1026.

Abbotsbury is best explored on foot. Use the signed car park at the eastern approach to the village. Turn left along Rodden Row, with its medley of stone and thatch or slate roofed 18th and 19th century listed cottages. Turn left again into Church Street. St Nicholas's has many interesting features including a stone effigy of an abbot in the porch; a 1638 chancel ceiling with beautiful plasterwork; gilded reredos and a fine brass chandelier. Continue down Church Street. Abbotsbury's abbey was largely destroyed during Henry VIII's Dissolution of the Monasteries (1536-40), but substantial ruins remain and some of its beautiful masonry has been re-used in other buildings. Abbey House, with its tearooms, stands on the site of the old monastic infirmary and is a case in point. Continue to the Tithe Barn, the most impressive monastic building to survive. One of the largest tithe barns in England at 272ft (82.5m) long, it dates from around 1400. Along with its ancient pond, it is now a children's farm.

Retrace your steps up Church Street and continue ahead along Market Street. Again, this is lined with listed buildings, the early 19th century Ilchester Arms being the most prominent. A footpath leads up to St Catherine's Chapel, which was probably built as a pilgrim chapel at about the same time as the Tithe Barn, around 1400. Perched boldly on its hill, it survived the Dissolution because it was a valuable seamark. Its buttresses and stone roof give an impression of mass and strength reinforced by the vaulted interior. Around it are medieval cultivation terraces, strip lynchets, best seen in evening light. The effort of climbing the hill is richly rewarded with a superb aerial view of Abbotsbury.

Abbotsbury's Swannery and Subtropical Gardens are two worthwhile extra visits. Keeping swans is an ancient tradition at Abbotsbury, where

Below top: The village from St Catherine's Hill and bottom: St Catherine's Chapel.

the Swannery has up to 600 birds and is the oldest managed swan population in the world. First recorded in 1393, it was established by Abbotsbury's Benedictine monks. After the Dissolution ownership passed to the Fox-Strangways family, the Earls of Ilchester, who own Abbotsbury village and estate. Abbotsbury's Subtropical Gardens are internationally famed for their camellias, magnolias, rhododendrons and hydrangeas.

Above: The pulpit in St Nicholas's. The arrow points to a hole caused by a musket ball during a skirmish in the Civil War!

Ashmore

Ashmore is reputed to be the highest village in Dorset at about 720 feet. The name derives from Old English; the pond (mere) where ash trees grow. The pond at the centre of the village may date from Roman times, a major Roman road passed close by connecting Bath and Badbury Rings. It is not natural, Ashmore sits on porous chalk, it is rather a dew pond lined with clay. Pretty greensand cottages surround the pond and green along with the imposing Manor House Farm.

At midsummer Ashmore holds the Filly Loo festival, celebrating the summer solstice and the filling of the pond. There's much dancing, good food and an appearance by the Green Man. Visitors are very welcome.

Close by is Compton Abbas Airfield, a small, charming grass airfield with a popular café where you can sit and watch planes taking off and landing.

Above: Two views across the village pond in Ashmore.

Bere Regis

St John's church is outstanding. Built in the East Dorset style of banded and chequerboarded flint, limestone and brick, it is particularly noted for its hammerbeam roof. Among the wonderfully carved and painted roof bosses are kings and saints, plus the twelve apostles. The nave arcade displays bizarre and humorous carvings, including a bear baiting monkey and a man suffering toothache. Also of note are the 16th century carved bench ends; the Skerne family brasses; the beautifully carved Norman font and the 1898 funeral bier. The once powerful Turbervilles too have monuments. They became extinct in the 18th century and their fate inspired Thomas Hardy to write his novel *Tess of the d'Urbervilles*.

Bere Regis's main street has some fine vernacular buildings, but some of the best examples are at the west end of the village in Shitterton. Meaning "farm at the end of the stream used as a sewer" the name is derived from plain Old English, but is sometimes rendered as Sitterton.

Left: The wonderful church roof. Above top: A thatched cottage in Shitterton, a small settlement attached to Bere Regis. Bottom: A detail of a carving on the nave arcade. This appears to be a man with a headache!

8

Burton Bradstock

Burton Bradstock is an exceptionally attractive village. Its stone built houses, many of them thatched, are prettily arranged around a network of lanes. A delight to explore on foot, it has two good pubs, the 17th century Three Horseshoes and the 19th century Anchor, noted for its fine windows. St Mary's has a list of rectors going back to 1295 and a particularly good wagon roof. The nave is 14th century, whilst the crossing, transepts and central tower date from the 16th century.

Cattistock

A large, handsome village, Cattistock has its own church, pub, post office/shop, tearoom and village hall. Many of its varied collection of listed buildings such as Pound House and Tailors Cottage in the Square are constructed of local stone and thatch. Others, equally

Above top: Cottages in Burton Bradstock.
Below left: Cattistock church.
Centre: Burton Bradstock church.
Below: The William Morris window in Cattistock church.

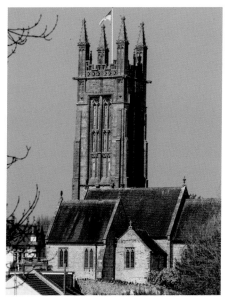

attractive, are in brick with slate roofs. Listed too is the Fox and Hounds, Cattistock's large, friendly village inn which dates from the 17th century and is built of chalk blocks on a rubble stone plinth. Within are flagged floors; an ancient wooden screen, exposed beams and a cavernous fireplace, as well as many curiosities such as the lifebelt from HMS Cattistock and the old pub sign. The Fox and Hounds has won several Taste of Dorset awards (proudly displayed under a sign "Old Farts' Corner") and is named after the Cattistock Hunt, nicknamed "True Blue" to honour its royal supporter, George III.

Buildings historian Nikolaus Pevsner described Cattistock's Grade I listed church as "the masterpiece amongst Dorset churches" of the 19th century. It is the work of Sir George Gilbert Scott and his eponymous son. Of especial note are the magnificent Perpendicular-styled tower; the baptistery with its wall and ceiling paintings and the delightful William Morris window.

Cerne Abbas

Cerne Abbas, Thomas Hardy's Abbot's Cernel, is named from the River Cerne and the Benedictine monastery founded in 987. It has an intriguing medley of historic buildings in stone, brick and flint banding with slate, thatch and tiled roofs. No less than 77 are listed, including the surviving abbey buildings, the church and Cerne's three inns, making the village ideal for a leisurely exploration on foot.

Above: The view from Giant Hill.

Pick up a heritage leaflet at Cerne Abbas Stores in Long Street and study the wall map beside it and the Abbot's Tearoom. Head to the Royal Oak, a 16th century inn with 18th and 19th century alterations. Features include period photographs, exposed beams, flagstones and an open fire.

Turn up Abbey Street, where the timber framed former Abbey tenements are also 16th century. St Mary's opposite was originally built by the monks about 1300. It has many interesting features, including medieval and 17th century wall paintings, a splendid Jacobean pulpit and a 15th century stone screen. Well-illustrated plaques describe the village's history.

The house called Cerne Abbey at the end of Abbey Street incorporates parts of the medieval monastic gatehouse, but was largely rebuilt from the 18th century. In its grounds (small admission fee) is the Abbot's Porch (c1500), noted for its lovely oriel window and embellished with several coats of arms and heraldic carvings. It and the Abbey Guest House are the only elements of Cerne Abbey to survive Henry VIII's Dissolution of Monasteries in 1539.

Divert into the nearby graveyard to see St Augustine's well, which is said to have healing properties. Legend has it that, like Moses striking the rock with his staff, St Augustine of Canterbury struck the ground causing a spring to issue forth during his great mission to convert the English between 596 and 605 CE.

Return to Long Street. Turn right past the handsome red brick Giant Inn to the New Inn. An impressive late 17th/18th century coaching inn with a large carriage entrance, it incorporates brick, Ham Stone, knapped flint and chalk block with a stone slate roof.

Continue down Long Street past the telephone booth. Turn left "Barton Meadows Farm" to view the medieval tithe barn (please keep to the footpath and respect the owner's privacy). Retrace your steps towards the start. Divert up Duck Street to the Giant Viewpoint.

Cerne's Giant is unmistakably a triumphant phallic symbol. Cut into the chalk, he is 180ft long, 167ft wide and brandishes a club 120ft long. His age and origins have been much debated. Although the earliest record of the Giant dates from 1742, he may be Romano-British, perhaps a British Hercules, though possibly his pagan roots are even older. However, recent archaeological research indicates the Giant is medieval, perhaps the 7th or 8th centuries CE. Possibly, Cerne Abbey was founded only 500m distant as a Christian counterblast to this virile Pagan symbol. The debate continues.

Left: Houses in Abbey Street.
Above top: The famous Cerne Abbas Giant.
Below: The medieval tithe barn.

The Abbot's Porch at Cerne Abbey.

Charminster

The older part of Charminster is clustered around its beautiful parish church and up East Hill, with a mix of vernacular buildings in thatch, stone, flint and brick. Although St Mary's tower is Tudor, the chancel arch and the pillars and arches in the nave are late Norman, as is the font, some of the walls and four small windows.

Flowing by the churchyard, the River Cerne is crossed by a stone bridge, one of several in Dorset bearing a plaque from the early 19th century threatening transportation for life to "any person wilfully injuring" it. Just upstream is an attractive modern footbridge, a peaceful place where three footpaths meet.

Follow East Hill into Westleaze to visit Wolfeton House, a handsome Grade 1 listed manor house with splendid plasterwork and panelling. Open to the public (check opening times before visiting), it dates from the 16th century, but with Victorian extensions and alterations.

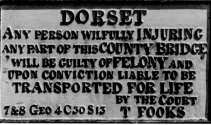

Above Top: The footbridge over the River Cerne. Middle: The sign on the bridge over the river.
Bottom: Wolfeton House.
Below and opposite: Charmouth Beach.

Charmouth

Charmouth's most prominent feature is its main axis, The Street, originally part of a Roman road which connected Exeter, Dorchester and Salisbury. Recovering from devastating Viking raids, Charmouth grew, like neighbouring Lyme, with the salt trade and fishing. It was granted a market and fair in 1278 and became a borough in 1297.

The village entered its golden age in 1758 when the Western Turnpike was completed. Seven or eight coaches

passed daily through The Street, which has many fine buildings, among them The George, a handsome coaching inn. Opposite is Abbot's House Restaurant, where a plaque declares Charles II slept there September 22-23, 1651 following his escape from the Battle of Worcester. He planned to take ship to St Malo with local shipmaster, Stephen Limbry. Hearing of this, Limbry's wife locked her husband in their bedroom and stole his clothes. Charles escaped eastwards, pursued by troops, eventually reaching France.

Charmouth beach is famed for fossils and its Heritage Coast Centre provides information on fossils, and local wildlife, plus fossil collecting and rockpooling walks throughout the year. Its fossil collections showcase recent finds and the stories behind them. Outstanding are the splendid ammonites and a woolly mammoth tooth discovered by an eight year old boy. Beneath the Heritage Centre is the Charmouth Fossil Shop, with an impressive range of local and imported fossils. Of special note is the ichthyosaur skull discovered in 2000 on the beach.

Chideock and Seatown

Straddling the A35, Chideock's main street is lined with handsome thatched buildings in warm gold brown local stone. Among the best are Chideock House Hotel and Chideock's two inns, the Clock and the George. All three are listed 17th century buildings. Chideock's parish church is also built of local stone. Dating from the 14/15th century, it was restored in 1880 and has a fine black marble monument to Sir John Chideock, builder of Chideock Castle, the ruins of which stand beyond Ruins Lane. Built in 1380, it was taken and retaken several times during the Civil War, before its destruction was ordered. Some imagination is needed to picture it as it was. However, the moat and several humps and bumps in the ground remain to show its outline. Within is a cross and memorial to five local Catholic martyrs, executed during Elizabeth I's reign.

Nearby Seatown has a 2km (1 ¼ mile) long shingle beach. Its historic inn, the Anchor, has a superb collection of local period and recent photographs, plus fossil items recovered from shipwrecks. A mile long hike leads to

Charmouth

Chideock

Golden Cap, at 191m (630ft) the highest cliff on England's South Coast and a wonderful viewpoint. This was to the advantage of both "preventives" and smugglers in the 18th and early 19th centuries, when smuggling was rife on the Dorset coast.

In 1880 Rev. T Worthington, curate of Chideock, wrote: "There used to be 30 to 40 fishermen at Seatown ostensibly employed in their lawful avocation, but really in smuggling. Not the fishermen only, but as in other seaside places half a century ago, the inhabitants in general were implicated in this contraband traffic, of which the sin in their eyes consisted only in being found out."

Knowing this, the government stationed an exciseman nearby from 1750. This close knit community relied heavily on the "Free Trade" and excisemen were deeply resented. One was shot dead at the top of the Anchor's stairs as he eavesdropped on smugglers below. His ghost is said to haunt the inn.

Above top: The George Inn, Chideock. Below: Seatown, showing the Anchor Inn.
Below left: The sign at the Anchor Inn.

Corfe Castle

Even in ruin, Corfe Castle dominates the village that bears its name. A natural defensive site, it occupies a high rocky hill with steep sides and guards a gap in the chalk ridge, the obvious gateway to the Isle of Purbeck. It probably began as a pre-Saxon site and was extended, modernised and strengthened by Saxon and, particularly, by Norman castle builders. It withstood sieges in 1138 and 1139 and was tested again during the Civil War, when Lady Mary Bankes's 80 defenders successfully held the castle against 500-600 Parliamentarians. Lady Mary held the castle dur-

ing a second siege in 1645 until one of her own officers treacherously admitted enemy soldiers. It subsequently took Parliamentarian sappers several months and a great deal of explosive to slight Corfe Castle and render it indefensible. The castle and the nearby tearooms and shop selling gifts and books are open through the National Trust.

The village has a wealth of handsome buildings in Purbeck stone with stone roofs. Over 200 are listed, including the village inns: the Greyhound, the Bankes Arms, the Fox and the Castle Inn. Also listed are the Post Office/shop and the Old Town Hall, which claims to be the smallest of its type in England. It houses the museum containing fossils, mason's tools, period clothing and photographs and a variety of commercial and domestic artefacts.

The parish church is largely Victorian, but with a 15th century tower. It is dedicated to St Edward, who was murdered at Corfe Castle in 978. Although he was the eldest son of King Edgar, who died in 975, and his acknowledged heir, Edward's claim to the throne was contested by his younger half-brother, Ethelred and by his step-mother, Elfrida. Who committed the deed is uncertain, but a large painting of Edward in the Square is captioned: "Edward the Martyr King of Wessex treacherously stabbed at Corfe's Gate in AD978 by his step-mother Elfrida."

Corfe Castle's railway station is beautifully restored in 1950s Southern Railway style. It too is listed and part of the 5½ mile long Swanage Railway, a very attractive heritage line which runs popular steam and vintage diesel hauled trains between Norden, Corfe Castle and Swanage using vintage carriages, including observation and dining cars.

Below left: The Bankes Arms.
Below: The castle and the village.

*A train pulling in to Corfe Castle
Station and, inset, the signal box.*

Cranborne

Cranborne was once of considerable importance with a weekly market and an abbey (later priory) founded in 980. The priory has gone, but its centre, the mainly medieval parish church, remains. Built of flint with stone bands, it is noted for its medieval wall paintings; 14/15th century carved pulpit with emblems of the chase; 13th century Purbeck stone font and finely painted Victorian chancel arch.

In Thomas Hardy's novel *Tess of the d'Urbervilles*, Cranborne is "Chaseborough" and the Fleur de Lys the "Flower-de-Luce" where Tess and her friends made merry. Although altered at various periods, this 16th century inn retains interesting features, including moulded ceiling beams, a large fireplace and period photographs.

Village guides are available at the bookshop opposite the inn, which stocks a range of new and used books, many on Dorset history. Follow the guide for a pleasant stroll around Cranborne, which has a medley of brick and brick and flint houses, many of them listed.

Above top: Cranborne Castle.
Below: The Fleur de Lys.

Cranborne's Garden Centre is open daily with a range of shrubs, trees, flowers and plants. Beyond are Cranborne Manor Gardens (open Wednesday afternoon in summer months) and beautiful Cranborne Manor (not open to the public). The original manor was built in the twelfth century as a hunting lodge for King John, while the present structure was built for Robert Cecil the first Earl of Salisbury in the early seventeenth century. The earl's principle residence is Hatfield House and the manor is usually the home of the heir to the estate, Viscount Cranborne.

A short stroll along Castle Hill Lane at the eastern end of the village will take you to Cranborne Castle, a Norman motte and bailey castle once topped by timber walls and buildings.

Above: Cranborne Manor.

Evershot

Parts of Thomas Hardy's *Tess of the D'Urbervilles* are set in and around Evershot. Tess breakfasted at Tess Cottage by the church on her way to meet Angel Clare's parents, whilst the Acorn Inn is called the Sow and Acorn by Hardy. The welcoming bar of this handsome coaching inn has a large stone fireplace with a heavy wooden lintel and a superb collection of local period photographs on the wall, showing Evershot and its street of stone built houses remarkably little changed. There are also many contemporary photographs of local people and a slate recording the achievements of yard of ale drinkers. Times for consuming some 2½ pints of ale in this fashion range from the champion's nine seconds to a rather less impressive 23 minutes 42 seconds.

As well as the Acorn (the only survivor of the six pubs Evershot once had), the village is fortunate in having a shop, bakery, school, village hall and Summer Lodge, a splendid country house hotel. Its church, St Osmond's, was largely rebuilt in the 19th century, but following the style of the 15th. Of special note is its brass showing Rector William Grey bearing a chalice.

Below left: The Acorn Inn, Evershot.
Above: Tess Cottage, Evershot.

Fiddleford

Fiddleford "has the most spectacular medieval manor house interior in Dorset" according to buildings historian Nikolaus Pevsner. (Open daily, English Heritage). Completed about 1370, it has undergone many changes since; the timber roofs of the great hall and solar are particularly impressive. It was probably built for William Latimer, Sheriff of Somerset and Dorset. His private residence comprises the buttery and pantry on the ground floor and the solar (large chamber) above. Latimer would have used the great hall for his official duties.

The adjacent watermill has a delightful view onto the River Stour. Both mill and manor were well known to smuggler Roger Ridout (1736-1811), who used Fiddleford Manor to store contraband. An account of 1895 describes "a string of horses with contraband in the narrow road between Okeford Fitzpaine and Fiddleford. One or two men armed in the front, then ten or twelve horses connected by ropes followed at a hard trot, and two

or three men brought up the rear. This cavalcade did not stop for any person… The contraband goods were principally brought from Lulworth and the coast, through Okeford Fitzpaine to Fiddleford, and thus distributed."

Following Ridout (who rests in Okeford Fitzpaine's churchyard, page 26), take the pretty lane through Fiddleford, passing several listed buildings dating from the 16-18th centuries. Fiddleford Inn is also listed. Built in the early 19th century it has exposed beams and a large carriageway (now infilled) with a bull's eye window above.

Langton Matravers

Langton Matravers is largely built of local Purbeck Stone. Many of the older buildings are listed, including the 18th century King's Arms which doubles as village store and café. Typically, it has stone roof brads and stone flagged floors. There are local period photographs in the bar and an attractive beer garden.

The statue of a mason stands in St George's churchyard. Behind the church is the Purbeck Stone Museum. In the yard stands a capstan of the type used with a winch to haul stone up the cliffs from nearby coastal quarries such as Dancing Ledge, Seacombe and Winspit, which are all accessible from the Coastpath between Langton and Worth Matravers (page 42). To visit them, park at Spyway in Langton as signed or at Worth and follow signed paths.

Smugglers sometimes used coastal quarries when unloading contraband. A large cargo of brandy was unloaded at Dancing Ledge in the 1790s and taken to Spyway Farm for storage. Later, it was transferred to Langton Matravers Church and secreted in the roof. Tragically, the roof gave way during a service. One worshipper was killed and several severely injured.

Smuggling continued into the 19th century. Quarry owner and churchwarden Charles Hayward again used the roof void to hide contraband

Left top: Fiddleford Manor.
Middle: Inside the manor.
Bottom: The River Stour by the mill.

brandy barrels. The weight of this extra spiritual presence rendered the walls unsafe and the church, with the exception of its 15th century tower, was rebuilt for the third time in 1875-6. Hayward's grandson, who acted as lookout, kept a diary describing the smuggling operation which still exists today. Charles Hayward's memorial plaque stands over the vestry door.

Above: A capstan or 'whim' at the Purbeck Stone Museum.

Littlebredy

This quiet 'out of the way' little village sits at the head of the Bride Valley and at the foot of the Valley of the Stones Nature Reserve. The stones in question are sarsen stones, from a layer of silicified sands and gravels broken up by repeated freezing in the last Ice Age. They have been used in the many nearby Neolithic stone circles and long barrows.

The village was once owned by the Abbey of Cerne and was sold after the Dissolution of the Monasteries. It is a rare example of an 'estate village' completely unspoilt by modern devel-

Left top: Dancing Ledge.
Bottom: The statue of a mason.

Above: Littlebredy church.

opment. The manor was bought by a wealthy banker in 1797 and has remained in the family ever since. The present manor house, Bride House, is early 19th century. The parkland behind the house and near the church is open for the public to enjoy and includes a lake with a charming waterfall.

Loders and Uploders

Loders has a splendid main street of thatched houses in warm golden stone. Many are listed, including Oak Cottage (number 17), which bears a 1755 datestone. Also listed is the early 19th century Loders Arms, which has an excellent doubled sided pub sign, period photographs, a log fire and a beer garden. Uploders, a mile further along the Asker valley has a pub too. The Crown is part of a delightful medley of stone buildings, some thatched, others slated or tiled.

Loders Court, Loders's handsome Georgian manor house, stands next to Loders parish church. The church's long history, including its time as a priory church, and many interesting features are explained by plaques in the porch. It has Norman elements, including the font. The nave is 13th century, whilst the 14th century west tower has embattled parapets and gargoyles. Also of note is the lovely modern altar frontal.

Above: A thatched cottage on Loders's lovely main street.

Above top to bottom: Bride House, Bride Park and the waterfall.

Marnhull

Marnhull is "Marlott", the "dispersed village" on Thomas Hardy's novel *Tess of the d'Urbervilles* and the heroine's birthplace. More a collection of hamlets than a nucleated village, it has three churches, several shops, a garage, a pharmacy and two pubs. Among its medley of historic and modern houses is Nash Court (not to be confused with the farmhouse opposite), given by Henry VIII to his last wife, Katherine Parr.

At the southern end of Marnhull is Hardy's "Pure Drop Inn", the thatched and oldest part of the Crown Inn, which is over 400 years old, with various additions and alterations over the centuries. Its features include two large open fires, both with heavy wood-

Above top: Marnhull, The Pure Drop Inn.
Below: Nash Court Farmhouse, Marnhull.

en lintels and one with a cast iron range. There is also extensive wooden panelling, a priest hole, flagstone floors and exposed beams, as well as a wide variety of period photographs.

Close to the Crown is St Gregory's, a handsome mainly 14th century church, with a fine nave roof and late medieval wall paintings. The alabaster Cherent tomb dates from around 1470.

Possibly the model for Hardy's "Rolliver's Inn", the Blackmore Vale Inn is at the opposite end of Marnhull and shows Tess on the façade. Thought to have begun as three cottages, it retains older elements, including a large fireplace, though it was rebuilt in 1913.

Melbury Osmond

Jemima Hand, Thomas Hardy's mother lived at 1 Barton Cottages behind the church and married the author's father here, whilst Melbury Osmond is Hardy's "Little Hintock" in *The Woodlanders*, the heroine of which is Grace Melbury. Furthermore, the large and magnificent Melbury House, seat of the Strangways family since 1500, appears as "King's Hintock Court" in "The Duke's Reappearance", Hardy's story that incorporates the legend that the Duke of Monmouth took refuge in Monmouth Cottage.

A walk down the village street from the church to Town End via the Watersplash, Packhorse Bridge and Monmouth Cottage passes a fine assortment of stone and thatch houses. The walk may be continued for a mile to Melbury House, by following the drive (a private road, but public footpath) through the park designed by Capability Brown and planted with fine trees. Beyond the house (normally closed to the public) the drive passes through the deer park, where fallow deer are often seen and on for another mile to Evershot (page 18).

Above top: Melbury House.
Below: Deer in the parkland of the house.

Milton Abbas

Milton Abbas was architect designed on the orders of Joseph Damer, the Earl of Dorchester, as a replacement for the original market town of Milton Abbas, which Damer demolished between 1771 and 1790. Capability Brown redesigned the Abbey site and Sir William Chambers built the new Milton Abbas in the neighbouring valley where Damer could not see it.

In contrast to the medley of styles and building materials found in many Dorset villages, Milton Abbas's identical, neatly spaced thatched cottages have the unity and orderliness of Georgian architecture. Also of a piece is the village inn, and church. However, the Almshouses with their Tuscan and Corinthian columns are distinctly different. They were built in the old town,

Above top: Melbury Osmond church.
Middle: A cottage in Melbury Osmond.
Below: The 'main' street in Melbury Osmond.

dismantled and re-erected here in 1779. A footpath from the foot of the village leads to the abbey church, which survived Henry VIII's Dissolution because the townspeople adopted it as their parish church. Among its many interesting features are the superb Jesse window designed by Augustus Pugin and the monument ordered by Joseph Damer to commemorate his wife, Caroline.

Milton Abbey forms the centre piece of Milton Abbey School, which occupies Damer's former country house. Built between 1771 and 1776 of ashlar stone with slate and lead roofs, it is a splendid complement to the abbey's church. Both buildings are Grade 1 listed.

Below: Milton Abbey from St Catherine's Chapel, reached by a short footpath from the school drive.

Above top: A typical cottage in Milton Abbas.
Middle: Milton Abbey and the school, Joseph Damer's mansion.
Bottom: The Hambro Arms, Milton Abbas.

Moreton

St Nicholas Church, Moreton, has an outstanding collection of engraved glass windows by Sir Laurence Whistler. The Georgian church dates from 1776, but was badly bomb damaged in 1940. It was a bold and imaginative decision to install modern glass (the last Whistler window was dedicated in 1985), bathing the church in light.

In 1935 the funeral of T.E. Lawrence was held at the church. Lawrence had died aged only 46, after swerving to avoid two pedestrians whilst he was riding his beloved Brough Superior motorcycle. Among the literary and political figures present were Robert Graves, Siegfried Sassoon, General A.P. Wavell, Lady Nancy Astor and Winston and Clementine Churchill. All had known him well. Lawrence's funeral also drew the national press. Perhaps inevitably a series of conspiracy theories about his untimely death arose which persist to the present day. After winning acclaim for his part in the Arab Revolt of 1916-18 and his account of the same in *The Seven Pillars of Wisdom*, Colonel Lawrence enlisted in the ranks of first the RAF and later the Tank Corps. Off duty, he retreated to Clouds Hill, a small cottage near Moreton, which he redesigned. It has many souvenirs of his life. Open through the National Trust it is on the 3¾ mile Lawrence Trail, shown on a plaque outside the church, along with more information about this fascinating man.

He lies buried at Moreton Cemetery (his grave is at the far end on the right). Next to the cemetery, Moreton's Walled Gardens have a wide variety of flowers, shrubs and trees. A delightful place to wander in and explore at leisure, they also contain sculptures, a café, children's play area and farm animals.

Below: Moreton church and its windows.

Nether Compton

Nether Compton is a compact and attractive stone built village, easy to explore on foot, with many listed buildings, including the 13th century church. Also of note is the Griffin's Head, with its 1599 datestone and old stone inglenook fireplace. Nearby Lower Dairy Farmhouse bears another datestone, 1661. However, the large pair of estate cottages on the village green are Victorian, 1893, as is the Old School and attached Schoolmaster's House, 1843.

Above: Nether Compton.

Okeford Fitzpaine

Okeford Fitzpaine's attractive, interesting and varied collection of vernacular buildings in stone and flint banding, brick, cob, thatch and slate meld together harmoniously. St Lo Farmhouse in the village centre at the Cross dates from the 16th century with later additions and alterations and is a good example of this eclectic choice of materials, as are the charming houses on the raised pavement opposite.

Built of brick, the Royal Oak in Lower Street is early 19th century and was the place where the Great Dorset Steam Fair (now at Tarrant Hinton,

page 34) was born. It is one of four buildings in the village to gain a blue plaque in 2022, the other being 75 the Cross; Rectory Cottage, Higher Street and the Rectory. Period photographs in the bar show the Royal Oak essentially unchanged, an impression reinforced by the museum's extensive collection of historic village photographs. Standing next to the village shop in the Cross, the museum also has a fire engine of 1895 and a funeral bier.

Look down from the Cross for a fine view of St Andrew's medieval church tower. In the churchyard, just west of the tower is the tomb of local smuggler Roger Ridout.

Above top: Okeford Fitzpaine and the church of St Andrew.
Below: The Royal Oak.

Pamphill

Pamphill is a scattered settlement, loosely based around its huge village green. Cared for by the National Trust, the green is shaded by mature oaks and features a cricket field with a thatched pavilion. The car park on the green has a helpful map, showing the footpaths and quiet lanes which can be explored on foot.

There is a good variety of vernacular buildings to be seen on a circular walk of approximately 4.5km/2¾ miles. Just south of the green is the delightful Vine Inn, its small bar and lounge like someone's living room. It has an excellent collection of local period photographs and a beer garden where vines grow around the trellis.

Above: The Vine, Pamphill.

Cowgrove Road car park gives access to Eyebridge and a pleasant stroll along the River Stour. Several thatched farmhouses and cottages face Cowgrove Road. Take the footpath by Poplar Farm and turn right onto All Fools Lane by brick cottages. At the far end of the lane, Joule Signs and Design produce slate signs and wire sculptures. A short diversion to the left leads to Abbot Street Forge, where handcrafted wrought ironwork is created. Follow the lane east towards the green to the Arts and Craft church, or continue further for Pamphill Dairy Parlour Café and Farm Shop.

Above: The River Stour at Eyebridge.

Powerstock

Powerstock's buildings, some thatched, some slated, some modern, some 17th, 18th and 19th century, are set in pleasingly random order amidst knolls and trees. In the centre is St Mary's church, noted for its richly ornamented chancel arch, one of the finest in Dorset and its 15th century south doorway with carved images of the Virgin and Child. In the churchyard near the south porch is a dole table, a very rare 13th century survival of the ancient custom of placing doles of bread for the poor – a precursor of the food bank (photo below).

Opposite the church is the Three Horseshoes, a comfortable Victorian inn with fine views. The Marquis of Lorne is a short walk or drive across the valley in the equally charming hamlet of Nettlecombe. This listed early 19th century stone built inn has a good collection of local period photographs.

Above: The village of Powerstock.

Puddletown

Puddletown is "Weatherbury" in Thomas Hardy's novels. It was recorded as Pidleton in 1212, meaning "farmstead on the river Piddle". Proposals to rename the village "Piddletown" in 1956 met with fierce local protests. Although much of Puddletown was rebuilt in the 1860s, it retains a good medley of vernacular buildings, mainly in Mill Street and the Square. Many are thatched.

St Mary's church, setting for several scenes in Hardy's *Far From the Madding Crowd*, has a splendid 17th century musicians' gallery, a largely unspoilt example of the gallery at Stinsford that played a notable part in Hardy's life (page 29). The medieval monuments of knights and a lady are interesting.

Athelhampton House on the Tolpuddle road dates from the 15th century and is a good example of a late medieval fortified manor. It and its gardens are open to the public. The Great Hall, with its timbered roof and musicians' gallery is especially fine.

Above top: Inside St Mary's Church, Puddletown.
Below: Athelhampton House.

Stinsford

Thomas Hardy was born in the Stinsford hamlet of Higher Bockhampton in 1840 in the cob and thatch family home, built by his great-grandfather* and his heart was buried in Stinsford churchyard when he died in 1928. The village was central to Hardy's life and writing and appears thinly disguised as "Mellstock" in *Far From the Madding Crowd, The Mayor of Casterbridge, Tess of the d'Urbervilles* and *Jude the Obscure.*

Hardy retained a lifelong interest in Stinsford's 13th century church, "the most hallowed place on earth" for him according to his second wife, Florence. He worshipped there as a boy and his father, uncle and grandfather all played and sang in the gallery – before it was replaced by a harmonium in 1840.

Hardy's sonnet, "A Church Romance", describes the first real-life encounter in 1835 between his mother, Jemima, as she sat in the Stinsford congregation and Hardy's father, a "minstrel, ardent, young and trim" in the gallery above.

"Mellstock" church and its musicians also have a key role in Hardy's first novel, *Under the Greenwood Tree.* Hardy later wrote : "This story of the Mellstock Quire and its old established west-gallery musicians ... is intended to be a fairly true picture, at first hand, of the personages, ways, and customs which were common among such orchestral bodies in the villages of fifty or sixty years ago."

*Hardy's Cottage is open through the National Trust. Pre-booked visits only.

Above top: The grave of Thomas Hardy's heart.
Below: Stinsford church.

Above top: Hardy's cottage.
Below: The bridge over the River Frome. at nearby Lower Bockhampton.

Stoke Abbott

Stoke Abbott's name tells its history as an outlying manor of Sherborne Abbey. Well sheltered beneath a ring of hills, including Lewesdon (915ft/279m) and Waddon Hill with the extant ramparts of its Roman fort, this exceptionally attractive village includes some 65 houses and cottages, most built in local stone. They mainly date from the 18th and 19th centuries and many are thatched, including Manor Farmhouse with its handsome mullioned windows.

Above: The Norman font in Stoke Abbott's church. Left: Manor Farmhouse.

The New Inn began as a farmhouse. As is often the case with inns called "New", the building is old and was renamed later in its history. Mainly 18th century with earlier elements, it is built of rubble and dressed stone walls and also has a fine thatched roof. Sold in 1854, it became a beer house, later an inn and is now Stoke Abbott's only pub. Opposite is Anchor House. First mentioned in 1759, it was the Anchor Inn until 1958 and a shop until 1973.

The parish church has a 12th/13th century core, with a 14th century porch and a solid, square 15th century tower. Its beautifully carved Norman font is thought to represent Noah, his sons and their wives.

Sturminster Marshall

Sturminster Marshall is best approached from the east, via White Mill. An 18th century corn mill rebuilt in 1776 on a site marked in the Domesday Book (1086), White Mill retains its original elm and applewood machinery. Unfortunately, this is too fragile to be used, but visitors have a guided tour. (National Trust 01258 858051).

Cross White Mill Bridge, said to be the oldest bridge in Dorset. Its timber pilings have been carbon dated to the 12th century, though what we see today is probably 16th century with later alterations. A metal plaque on the bridge (1827) warns that anyone wilfully damaging it risks being transported for life.

Sturminster's brown and grey stone church is partly medieval, partly Victorian. In the south porch are two medieval coffin lids. Opposite is the Red Lion, where local period photographs show the village as it was over a century ago. A short walk leads to the village green, around which are a scattering of listed historic buildings, several thatched.

Sydling St Nicholas

Sydling St Nicholas is a long village nestled in a beautiful chalk stream valley. Take a stroll along its main street and loop back along the pretty footpath by Sydling Water to appreciate its pleasing medley of vernacular buildings in stone and flint banding, brick, thatch and slate. Stop at the Greyhound and study the excellent collection of local period photographs, showing village life of a century and more ago. One is of a man and his greyhound and the rabbits they have hunted.

The mainly 15th century church of St Nicholas is built of rubble stone and flint with Ham stone dressings. Within, St Nicholas's has a fine wagon roof and many baroque monuments. John Schlesinger used the churchyard in his 1967 film of Thomas Hardy's *Far From the Madding Crowd* for the scenes where Fanny Robin is buried and Sergeant Troy comes to mourn her. On the far side of the churchyard is a huge tithe barn with pigeon holes at one end.

Above: The path by Sydling Water.

Symondsbury

A large, handsome village, Symondsbury shelters below Colmer's Hill, a distinctive conical landmark for miles around topped with Scots pines. The Ilchester Arms, its Grade II* listed thatched pub, has a 15th century core with 17th century and later alterations. Beyond is the Victorian school (1868) and the cruciform 14th century church of local stone with a barrel roof built by shipwrights from West Bay. Dorset's great folklorist, John Symonds Udal, a friend of Thomas Hardy, worshipped here and is buried in the churchyard.

Behind the church is Symonds-

Above: The Ilchester Arms and its colourful sign.

Above: Symondsbury from Colmer's Hill.

bury Estate's Manor Yard. Home to a variety of interesting shops, a café/restaurant and artisan workshops, it has free parking and is a delight to explore. The contemporary gallery housed in the 18th century former stables features art in various media from local artists, both new and established, including ceramics, wood carvings, textiles, photography and glass. The functions venue is converted from a medieval tithe barn. A signed footpath from the yard leads up Colmer's Hill.

The Tarrants

Eight villages lie along the Tarrant Valley. Joined by a quiet road, they make a pleasant twelve mile drive or cycle ride with much of interest. "Tarrant" is an old Celtic river name, a variant on "Trent". It rises near Tarrant Gunville, named after its 12/13th century Norman French owners, the Gundvilles. The village has a variety of vernacular buildings, some thatched, some in brick and flint banding, whilst the church is built in bands of stone and flint.

Driving south from Tarrant Gunville, note the once impressive gateway to Eastbury Park and Eastbury House. Designed by Sir John Vanbrugh, Eastbury took twenty years to build (1718-38) and was described as "one of the grandest and most superb houses in the county, indeed the kingdom". Alas, it proved impractically huge and expensive. Most of it was demolished in the late 18th century, but its handsome former service wing survived. A Grade 1 listed building; it may be occasionally glimpsed through the trees from public paths around the park.

Tarrant Hinton belonged to Shaftesbury Abbey from Anglo-Saxon times. It too has a pleasing medley of vernacular cottages and a handsome stone and flint church. Continue south through Tarrant Launceston. Cross the river Tarrant by a ford next to the handsome 17th century footbridge to explore Tarrant Monkton, a compact and unspoilt village with, yet again, several pleasing vernacular buildings, including its thatched inn. The 18th century Langton Arms has a superb collection of local period photographs showing farming in bygone days. Tarrant Rawston's flint and stone church stands behind Rawston Farm, itself a listed 16/17th century building. Drive on; then turn left and left again to find Tarrant Rushton's small medieval church, also in local stone and flint. Just to the east of Tarrant Rushton and accessed via the road to Witchampton lies the old Tarrant Rushton airfield. The perimeter track and two hangars remain as well as a poignant memorial. This was the airfield where the first gliders took off on

Above top: The gateway to Eastbury House. Middle: The bridge at Tarrant Monkton. Bottom: Cottages at Tarrant Gunville.

Above middle: Keyneston Mill. Bottom: The memorial at Tarrant Rushton airfield, an old hangar in the background.

the eve of D-Day 1944, carrying troops and equipment who would take part in the fight for Pegasus Bridge.

The True Lover's Knot at Tarrant Keyneston has a good collection of local period photographs. Several stories explain its possibly unique name. One is that the son of an early landlord fell in love with a Dorset noble's daughter. The noble was furious and forbade the match. Quite distraught, his daughter hanged herself. Overcome with grief, her lover took the same fatal course. Now a grieving, childless widower, the noble also hanged himself – hence the True Lover's Knot has three loops. In an equally tragic explanation, the daughter of an early landlord was raped by three men. He took his revenge by hanging them with one rope tied in "a true lover's knot". A third and more hopeful explanation is that the inn was named after the knots which secured the masts to sailing ships. Sailors sent miniature versions of these knots to their sweethearts. If they could untie the knot the romance would continue.

Continue through the village to Keyneston Mill. Visitors can explore the scented botanical gardens and 50 acre estate, where plants are grown and harvested for luxury perfumes. Plaques explain the properties of particular plants and the process of extracting scents. Keyneston Mill also hosts art exhibitions, special events and a bistro.

The turning for Tarrant Crawford is on the left, only 500m further on in the Shapwick direction, but easily missed as it is marked "Private drive for visitors to church only". St Mary's simple and evocative 12th century church stands alone amid the fields, shaded by trees. It is all that remains of Tarrant Abbey, a wealthy Cistercian nunnery, to which it may have been the lay chapel. Most of the nave's walls are covered in 14th century paintings. They include St Margaret of Antioch and three animated skeletons, who warn three princes of the emptiness of earthly rank and wealth. Though degraded, they give an impression of the warmth and colour that characterised England's medieval churches before Protestant iconoclasm.

Toller Fratrum

Toller Fratrum is an isolated hamlet at the end of a single track road, though it once had a larger population and roads, now paths, which lead to neighbouring villages. It has several historic buildings, including the 17th century Corner Cottages and Little Toller Farm, the manor house built in 1540 and restored after severe fire damage in 2015.

Most intriguing is the humble 19th century church of St Basil, a replacement for the much larger church where the Knights Hospitallers, who

Page 34: Little Toller Farm.
Above top: The church of St Basil.
Below: The Saxon font in the church.

once owned the manor, worshipped. Within is a truly remarkable and astonishing stone font. Carved sometime between the 8th and 12th centuries, it is most likely Saxon. Might it represent Christ and the Apostles, or possibly Moses exhorting the Israelites? It remains an enigma, though the equally striking figure above the altar is clearly Mary Magdalene in tears washing Christ's foot with her hair.

Curious too is the name "Toller". The old Celtic name for the River Hooke, it signifies "stream in a deep valley", whilst "Fratrum", means "of the brethren". However, neighbouring Toller Porcorum ("of the pigs") got its name from its herd of swine!

Tolpuddle

This quiet Dorset village has a proud place in British labour history as the home of the six "Tolpuddle Martyrs". National attention was focussed on Tolpuddle in 1834 when six local farm labourers were sentenced to seven years' transportation, nominally for swearing an illegal oath, in reality for forming a trade union and thus challenging the authority of landowners and magistrates, the rural Establishment. Their savage sentences caused a national outcry. After a three year long campaign the men were "pardoned" by King William IV. Their dramatic story and the harsh realities of 19th century life in rural Dorset are told in vivid detail with multi-media presentations in the Tolpuddle Martyrs Museum, from where visitors can follow the "Tolpuddle Martyrs Trail" around the village.

The trail (www.tolpuddlemartyrs.org.uk/trail) includes the grave of James Hammett (one of the six) in the churchyard and the Martyrs' Tree under which the friendly society they formed met. It continues past the Martyrs' Inn to Thomas Standfield's Cottage, where the six took the oath that got them convicted and on by the Methodist Chapel, successor to the one their leader, George Loveless, preached in. The trail ends by the Memorial Arch. This commemorates their history and is celebrated in the annual Tolpuddle Festival. Spread over three days, it includes speeches, live music and a variety of stalls and entertainments. It culminates in a lively procession through the village in which trade unionists from all over Britain, including a strong Dorset contingent, march with flags, banners, musicians and dancers.

> "WE HAVE INJURED NO MAN'S REPUTATION. CHARACTER. PERSON OR PROPERTY. WE WERE UNITING TOGETHER TO PRESERVE OUR-SELVES, OUR WIVES AND OUR CHILDREN FROM UTTER DECRADATION AND STARVATION".
> (GEORGE LOVELESS'S DEFENCE).

Above: A statement by George Loveless.
Below middle: A memorial seat to the martyrs and inset, the Methodist chapel and the Martyrs' tree.
Bottom left: James Hammett's grave.
Bottom right: The Tolpuddle Festival.

Trent

"There are few churches in Dorset with so much to enjoy," enthused buildings historian Nikolaus Pevsner, who particularly liked St Andrew's 14th century tower. Of especial note are the carved medieval bench ends; the beautiful carved screen; the baroque pulpit and the east window's stained glass, much of it German and Dutch.

Imagine Charles II's feelings in 1651 when he heard Trent's church bells mistakenly celebrating his capture and death following the Battle of Worcester. Having escaped Worcester in disguise, Charles was hiding by the church in Trent Manor, home of Colonel Francis Wyndham with a £1000 reward on his head and death to anyone hiding him. Charles later left Trent with Wyndham's niece, Juliana Coningsby. Posing as a runaway couple, they made for Charmouth, where Charles's attempt to flee to France was foiled (page 12). It is said that after the Restoration in 1660, Wyndham refused to allow any Trent parishioners to ring the church bells and had ringers over from Royalist Compton (page 26) instead.

An account of Charles's adventures and a proclamation for the "Discovery and Apprehending of Charls Stuart and other Traytors" is displayed in the Rose and Crown, along with more Stuart memorabilia. Trent's large 18/19th century inn also has two fine fireplaces and flagstone floors.

Right above: Trent church.
Middle: A lovely Trent house.
Bottom: The east window, Trent church.

Tyneham

The deserted village of Tyneham is a time capsule with its own poignant story. Along with the downland and coast between Lulworth and Kimmeridge, Tyneham was requisitioned by the Army and evacuated in 1943 to allow troops to train for the D Day landings in Normandy. Although the villagers were promised they could return after the Second World War was won, permission was refused. Tyneham and surrounding area remain under MOD control and public access is limited to most weekends and public holidays, but it is wise to check by calling 01929 404714 or visit www.tynehamopc.org.uk before visiting.

Tyneham church has been preserved with tableaux showing period photographs and memories of villagers and village life in the late 19th and early 20th centuries. Also preserved is the schoolhouse. Children's names mark the clothes pegs in the lobby. Old fashioned teaching aids hang on the classroom walls and samples of the children's work lie on the bench desks. It seems the school bell only rang an hour ago.

Ruined and roofless cottages too have tableaux telling the histories of the families who lived in them, along with photographs of them at work and play. Although the farmhouse has gone, Tyneham Farm remains, its hand tools, stables, horse drawn harrow and farm wagon a reminder of the recent past when men and horses rather than tractors and diesel machinery provided motive power.

Above top: Tyneham church.
Middle: Tyneham cottages.
Bottom: Inside Tyneham school, preserved as it was in 1943.
Overleaf: Post Office Row, Tyneham, the church in the background.

West Lulworth

West Lulworth's superb natural setting amid some of the finest scenery on the Jurassic Coast draws large numbers of visitors. Lulworth Cove itself is a near perfect circle of wonderfully clear water sheltered by spectacularly folded rocks. It is best viewed from the surrounding cliffs. Some visitors approach Lulworth by following the cliff path from Durdle Door, a striking limestone arch carved by the sea, a mile to the west. It's a stiff walk, but gives superb views of coast and village.

Roadside parking in Lulworth is limited, but there is a large car park (fee) by the beach. Next to it, the Heritage Centre (free entry) gives an excellent introduction to the area's world famous geology, as well as its history, archaeology and natural history with videos, photographs, fossils and rocks. The attached shop sells souvenirs and local interest books.

Lulworth's mile long main street leads past a pleasing medley of thatched and more modern buildings. From the ice cream and snack stalls on the beach to the thatched 18th century Castle Inn at the top end of the village, visitors are amply catered for with cafés, the Lulworth Cove Inn, a bistro, a restaurant, gift shops and a well-stocked village shop selling beach gear and beach wear. The pebble and sand beach is always popular, though much quieter off season. It is ideal for boating and swimming. Paddleboards and kayaks may be hired by the beach.

Opposite page: Looking towards Durdle Door from the coast path.
Above: Cottages at West Lulworth.
Right top: The path from Durdle Door to Lulworth Cove.

Whitchurch Canonicorum

Whitchurch Canonicorum's exceptionally impressive church is dedicated to St Candida (St Wite) and contains her shrine; an inscribed leaden casket housing the bones of a woman aged about forty. These are thought to be the only ancient relics in England apart from those of Edward the Confessor in Westminster to have survived the Reformation. The medieval church venerated St Wite as a martyr and pilgrims came to Whitchurch to seek her aid and healing, putting their diseased limbs in the openings at the base of her shrine. The church also has a Norman font, a Jacobean pulpit and monuments. Be sure not to miss St Wite's statue, lodged in a niche on the exterior of the tower.

Right middle: Whitchurch Canonicorum Church.
Right bottom: The statue of St Wite.

Winterborne Tomson

Only a hamlet, Winterborne Tomson is well worth visiting for its tiny Norman church, which was nearly lost to time and decay in the last century. St Andrew's was saved from ruin by a sale of Thomas Hardy's manuscripts in 1931. This has enabled a sensitive restoration which has preserved its charmingly simple features. These include the 18th century box pews and two decker pulpit with its tester; the wooden screen; wagon roof and west gallery. Hardy, a church architect, would certainly have approved.

Above: Winterborne Tomson's pretty church and its inside with box pews.

Right: The village pond and cottages in Worth Matravers.

Worth Matravers

Worth Matravers is a handsome Purbeck stone village. The Square and Compass, its delightfully old fashioned 18th century inn, serves beer from the barrel. Appropriately, the inn's sign bears a depiction of a square and a compass: essential mason's tools and the symbol of the Freemasons. The Square and Compass also has an excellent assortment of local period photographs and a small museum containing a remarkably large collection of local fossils.

Many of Worth's most attractive vernacular buildings, including its take-away teashop, are clustered around its duck pond and green. The church of St Nicholas is Norman with a striking chancel arch, strongly carved with zigzags. The arch is also a mystery: it is thought to have been brought here from elsewhere, possibly a dissolved monastery, but which one is not known. The

43

church is noted too for its fine Norman arch over the south door and Norman corbel tables.

A 45 minute walk from Worth leads by medieval strip lynchets (cultivation terraces) to Winspit Quarries, which may be explored with due care. The coastal views are superb. A mile further west along the Coastpath is St Aldhelm's Head, with its square medieval chapel and its memorial to the pioneering radar research carried out here in 1940-42.

Another diversion leads to 140 million year old dinosaur footprints at Keates Quarry. Start from the Square and Compass. Follow the lane towards Langton Matravers for 500m. Take the second footpath right, signed "Priest's Way". Continue east via fields, then into a broad track signed "Langton Matravers" and divert left as signed to see the footprints.

Bottom: The coast at Winspit.
Below left: Worth Matravers church.
Below right: Dinosaur footprints.

Yetminster

St Andrew's is a medieval church with several interesting features. The north aisle ceiling has paintings from circa 1460 and a fine monument from 1649. In the south aisle are carved capitals which each tell a story and also a restored brass to John Horsey and his lady.

Turn left down Yetminster's main street, which has a fine medley of stone built vernacular buildings from the 16th through to the 18th century. Many are listed, including the 17th century Manor House and Manor Farmhouse, as well as the 16-18th century White Hart.

Local folk music band the Yetties often played here in the skittle alley. This and the large main bar, which includes exposed beams, mullioned windows and a large fireplace with a wooden lintel, are being refurbished and have a variety of Yetties' photographs and memorabilia.

Further down the street, the Old School Gallery and Café bears a blue plaque to its founder, the chemist and physicist Robert Boyle (1627-91), who endowed it "for 20 poor boys of Yetminster, Leigh and Chetnole". Completed in 1697, it now serves home cooked food and exhibits and sells local art and crafts.

Right top: The brass to Sir John Horsey in St Andrew's.
Middle: The Old School Gallery and Café.
Bottom: Manor Farmhouse..